Table of Content

Chapter 1: What is AI?

Introduction to AI

Artificial Intelligence, commonly abbreviated as AI, is a branch of computer science dedicated to building smart machines capable of performing tasks that typically require human intelligence. These tasks include, but are not limited to, recognizing speech, making decisions, translating languages, and identifying patterns. AI's ultimate goal is to create systems that can function intelligently and independently, mimicking the cognitive functions of the human brain.

History of AI

The concept of AI is not new. Its roots can be traced back to ancient times, where myths and stories depicted artificial beings endowed with intelligence or consciousness by master craftsmen. However, AI as a scientific discipline was officially established in the mid-20th century. In 1956, John McCarthy, an American computer scientist, coined the term "artificial intelligence" and organized the Dartmouth Conference, which is considered the founding moment of AI as a field of research.

Core Concepts of AI

To understand AI, it is essential to grasp its core concepts:

- **Learning**: This is the process by which AI systems improve their performance over time. It can be further divided into supervised learning, unsupervised learning, and reinforcement learning.
    - Supervised Learning: Involves training an AI system using a labeled dataset. The system learns to predict outcomes based on input-output pairs.
    - Unsupervised Learning: Involves training an AI system using unlabeled data. The system tries to identify patterns and relationships within the data.
    - Reinforcement Learning: Involves training an AI system to make decisions by rewarding desired behaviors and punishing undesired ones.
- **Reasoning**: AI systems can process information and draw conclusions based on evidence or logical rules. This involves both deductive reasoning (deriving specific conclusions from general principles) and inductive reasoning (deriving general principles from specific observations).

- **Perception**: AI systems can interpret sensory input such as images, sounds, and touch. This capability is crucial for applications like image recognition, speech recognition, and natural language processing.
- **Language Understanding**: AI systems can understand and generate human language. This includes natural language processing (NLP), which enables machines to read, understand, and respond to human languages.
- **Problem Solving**: AI systems can solve complex problems by breaking them down into smaller, manageable components and applying various strategies to find solutions.

Types of AI

AI can be broadly categorized into two types: Narrow AI and General AI.

- **Narrow AI**: Also known as Weak AI, narrow AI is designed and trained to perform a specific task. These systems are highly specialized and can perform their designated tasks with a high degree of accuracy. Examples of narrow AI include virtual personal assistants like Siri and Alexa, recommendation systems used by Netflix and Amazon, and image recognition software used in medical diagnostics.

General AI: Also known as Strong AI or Artificial General Intelligence (AGI), general AI refers to systems that possess the ability to perform any intellectual task that a human can do. These systems would have general cognitive abilities, allowing them to learn and apply knowledge in different contexts. General AI remains a theoretical concept and has not yet been achieved.

Components of AI

The construction of AI involves several components, each playing a crucial role in the system's overall functionality:

- **Algorithms**: At the heart of AI systems are algorithms, which are sets of rules or instructions that guide the system in performing its tasks. These algorithms can process large amounts of data, recognize patterns, and make decisions based on the insights derived from the data.
- **Data**: Data is the fuel that powers AI systems. AI systems require vast amounts of data to learn and make accurate predictions or decisions. This data can come from various sources, including databases, sensors, and user inputs.

- **Computational Power**: AI systems require significant computational power to process data and run complex algorithms. Advances in computing hardware, such as Graphics Processing Units (GPUs) and Tensor Processing Units (TPUs), have enabled the development of more sophisticated AI systems.
- **Training and Testing**: AI systems need to be trained on large datasets to learn and improve their performance. This involves feeding the system with data and adjusting the algorithms based on the system's output. After training, the system is tested on new data to evaluate its performance and accuracy.

Applications of AI

AI has a wide range of applications across various industries, including:

- **Healthcare**: AI is revolutionizing healthcare by enabling early diagnosis of diseases, personalized treatment plans, and predictive analytics for patient care. AI-powered medical imaging systems can detect abnormalities in X-rays and MRIs with high accuracy, while AI algorithms can analyze genetic data to identify potential health risks.

- **Finance**: In the financial sector, AI is used for fraud detection, algorithmic trading, and customer service. AI systems can analyze transaction data to identify suspicious activities, execute trades based on market trends, and assist customers with their banking needs through chatbots.

- **Retail**: AI is transforming the retail industry by enhancing the shopping experience and optimizing supply chain management. AI-powered recommendation systems suggest products based on customer preferences, while AI algorithms analyze sales data to forecast demand and manage inventory.

- **Transportation**: AI is driving innovation in transportation with the development of autonomous vehicles and smart traffic management systems. Self-driving cars use AI to navigate roads, avoid obstacles, and make real-time decisions, while AI-powered traffic systems optimize traffic flow and reduce congestion.

- **Education**: AI is reshaping education by providing personalized learning experiences and automating administrative tasks. AI-powered educational platforms can adapt to individual learning styles and pace, while AI algorithms can grade assignments and manage student records.

Future of AI

The future of AI holds immense potential and promises to bring about significant advancements in various fields. Some of the key areas of development include:

- **AI in Space Exploration**: AI will play a crucial role in future space missions by assisting in navigation, data analysis, and autonomous decision-making. AI-powered robots and spacecraft will explore distant planets and moons, gather data, and perform scientific experiments.
- **AI in Climate Change Mitigation**: AI will be instrumental in addressing climate change by optimizing energy use, predicting weather patterns, and modeling the impacts of environmental policies. AI algorithms can analyze vast amounts of climate data to identify trends and inform decision-making.

- **AI in Advanced Manufacturing**: AI will drive the next wave of industrial revolution by enabling smart manufacturing systems. AI-powered robots and automation systems will enhance efficiency, quality control, and customization in manufacturing processes.

- **AI in Personalized Medicine**: AI will revolutionize healthcare by enabling highly personalized treatment plans based on individual genetic and lifestyle data. AI algorithms will analyze vast amounts of medical data to identify the most effective treatments for each patient.

- **AI in Human-Machine Collaboration**: The future will see increased collaboration between humans and AI systems, leading to the development of more intuitive and user-friendly interfaces. AI-powered assistants will enhance human capabilities and assist in complex decision-making processes.

Artificial Intelligence is a rapidly evolving field with the potential to transform every aspect of our lives. From healthcare and finance to transportation and education, AI is driving innovation and providing solutions to some of the world's most pressing challenges.

Chapter 2: How Does AI Work?

Introduction

Understanding how AI works involves delving into the various techniques and processes that allow machines to perform tasks that typically require human intelligence. AI encompasses a wide range of technologies, but the core principles revolve around learning, reasoning, and self-correction. This chapter will explore the fundamental concepts of data processing, machine learning, and deep learning, and explain the differences between generative AI, deep learning, and machine learning.

Data Processing in AI

Data is the lifeblood of AI systems. AI relies on vast amounts of data to learn and make informed decisions. Data processing involves several steps:

- **Data Collection**: Gathering raw data from various sources such as sensors, databases, and user inputs. This data can be structured (e.g., databases) or unstructured (e.g., text, images).

- **Data Cleaning**: Ensuring that the data is free from errors, inconsistencies, and duplicates. Cleaning the data is crucial for accurate AI predictions.

- **Data Transformation**: Converting the data into a format that can be easily processed by AI algorithms. This may involve normalizing values, encoding categorical variables, and scaling numerical data.

- **Data Storage**: Storing the processed data in databases or data lakes for easy access and retrieval by AI systems.

Machine Learning (ML)

Machine Learning is a subset of AI that focuses on developing algorithms that enable computers to learn from data and make predictions or decisions without being explicitly programmed. There are three main types of machine learning:

- **Supervised Learning**: In supervised learning, the AI system is trained on a labeled dataset, which means that each input comes with an associated output. The goal is to learn a mapping from inputs to outputs. Examples include classification (e.g., spam detection) and regression (e.g., predicting house prices).

- **Unsupervised Learning**: In unsupervised learning, the AI system is given unlabeled data and must find patterns or structures within the data. Common techniques include clustering (e.g., customer segmentation) and dimensionality reduction (e.g., principal component analysis).

- **Reinforcement Learning**: In reinforcement learning, the AI system learns by interacting with its environment and receiving feedback in the form of rewards or penalties. The goal is to learn a policy that maximizes cumulative rewards. Examples include game playing (e.g., AlphaGo) and robotic control.

Deep Learning

Deep Learning is a specialized subset of machine learning that uses neural networks with many layers (hence "deep") to model complex patterns in data. Neural networks are inspired by the structure and function of the human brain. Here are some key concepts in deep learning:

- **Neural Networks**: Composed of layers of interconnected nodes (neurons), where each node processes input and passes the output to the next layer. Common types of neural networks include feedforward neural networks, convolutional neural networks (CNNs) for image processing, and recurrent neural networks (RNNs) for sequential data.

- **Training Neural Networks**: Involves adjusting the weights of the connections between nodes to minimize the error between the predicted output and the actual output. This is typically done using a technique called backpropagation.

- **Activation Functions**: Non-linear functions applied at each node to introduce non-linearity into the network, allowing it to model complex relationships. Common activation functions include ReLU (Rectified Linear Unit), sigmoid, and tanh.
- **Optimization Algorithms**: Methods used to minimize the error during training, such as gradient descent and its variants (e.g., stochastic gradient descent, Adam).

Generative AI

Generative AI focuses on creating new content, such as images, music, or text, that is indistinguishable from human-generated content. This involves several techniques:

- **Generative Adversarial Networks (GANs)**: Consist of two neural networks, a generator and a discriminator, that are trained together. The generator creates fake data, and the discriminator evaluates its authenticity. The goal is to improve the generator until the fake data is indistinguishable from real data.

- **Variational Autoencoders (VAEs)**: Encode input data into a lower-dimensional representation and then decode it back to the original form. This helps in generating new data that is similar to the original data.
- **Transformers**: Used primarily in natural language processing (NLP), transformers like GPT-3 (Generative Pre-trained Transformer) generate human-like text by predicting the next word in a sequence based on the context provided by previous words.

Differences Between Generative AI, Deep Learning, and Machine Learning			
Feature	Generative AI	Deep Learning	Machine Learning
Definition	AI that can create new content	Subset of ML with neural networks	Broad field including many approaches
Examples	ChatGPT, DALL-E	Image/speech recognition	Predictive analytics, recommendation systems
Complexity	High	Very High	Moderate
Data Requirements	Massive amounts of diverse data	Large volumes of labeled data	Varies, but often large datasets
Computational Power	High	Extremely High	Varies
Application Focus	Creative tasks, content generation	Complex pattern recognition	Predictive modeling, classification, etc.
Key Techniques	GANs, VAEs, Transformers	Neural Networks (CNNs, RNNs)	Decision Trees, SVMs, Clustering

Real-World Examples of AI

Understanding how AI works can be further illustrated through real-world applications:

- **Healthcare**: AI algorithms are trained on medical imaging data to detect diseases such as cancer. For instance, convolutional neural networks (CNNs) are used to analyze X-rays, MRIs, and CT scans, providing doctors with early diagnosis and treatment options.

- **Finance**: Banks use AI to detect fraudulent transactions. Machine learning models analyze transaction patterns to identify anomalies that may indicate fraud. This helps in real-time monitoring and prevention of fraudulent activities.

- **Customer Service**: AI-powered chatbots and virtual assistants are trained using natural language processing (NLP) techniques to understand and respond to customer queries. This improves customer experience by providing instant support and resolving issues efficiently.

- **Autonomous Vehicles**: Self-driving cars use deep learning models to process data from cameras, LIDAR, and other sensors to navigate roads, recognize obstacles, and make driving decisions. Companies like Tesla and Waymo are at the forefront of developing this technology.

- **Entertainment**: Streaming services like Netflix use AI to recommend shows and movies based on users' viewing history. Machine learning algorithms analyze user preferences and behaviors to personalize recommendations, enhancing the user experience.

Challenges in AI

Despite the remarkable advancements, AI faces several challenges:

- Data Quality and Quantity: AI systems require large amounts of high-quality data to learn effectively. Obtaining and curating such data can be difficult, especially in domains where data is scarce or sensitive.

- Bias and Fairness: AI models can perpetuate and amplify biases present in the training data. Ensuring fairness and preventing discrimination requires careful design and evaluation of AI systems.

- **Explainability**: Many AI models, especially deep learning models, operate as "black boxes," making it difficult to understand how they arrive at their decisions. Improving the interpretability of AI models is crucial for building trust and ensuring accountability.

- **Security and Privacy**: AI systems can be vulnerable to attacks, such as adversarial examples where input data is intentionally manipulated to deceive the AI. Ensuring the security and privacy of AI systems is essential to prevent misuse and protect sensitive information.

- **Ethical Considerations**: The deployment of AI raises ethical questions about job displacement, autonomy, and the potential for AI to be used in harmful ways. Addressing these concerns requires collaboration between technologists, policymakers, and society at large.

Understanding how AI works is fundamental to appreciating its potential and addressing its challenges. AI relies on sophisticated algorithms, vast amounts of data, and powerful computational resources to perform tasks that typically require human intelligence. By leveraging machine learning and deep learning techniques, AI systems can learn from data, recognize patterns, and make informed decisions.

Generative AI, deep learning, and traditional machine learning each have unique characteristics and applications, contributing to the diverse landscape of AI technology. As AI continues to evolve, it is crucial to address the technical, ethical, and societal challenges to ensure that AI systems are beneficial, fair, and secure.

Chapter 3: Why AI is Important?

Introduction

Artificial Intelligence (AI) is more than just a technological advancement; it is a transformative force that is reshaping industries, driving innovation, and offering solutions to some of the most pressing challenges facing society today. This chapter delves into the reasons why AI is important, highlighting its impact on various sectors, its potential to enhance human capabilities, and the opportunities it presents for future development.

Enhancing Efficiency and Productivity

One of the most significant benefits of AI is its ability to enhance efficiency and productivity across various industries. AI systems can automate repetitive and mundane tasks, freeing up human workers to focus on more complex and creative activities. This automation leads to increased productivity, reduced operational costs, and improved accuracy.

- **Manufacturing**: AI-powered robots and automation systems streamline manufacturing processes, from assembly lines to quality control. These systems can work around the clock without breaks, increasing production rates and ensuring consistent product quality.

- **Customer service**: AI-driven chatbots and virtual assistants handle customer inquiries and support requests, providing instant responses and resolving issues efficiently. This not only improves customer satisfaction but also allows human agents to focus on more complex customer interactions.

- **Data Analysis**: AI systems can process and analyze vast amounts of data much faster than humans, identifying patterns, trends, and insights that can inform decision-making. This capability is particularly valuable in industries like finance, healthcare, and marketing, where data-driven insights are crucial for success.

Improving Decision Making

AI enhances decision-making processes by providing accurate, data-driven insights. AI algorithms can analyze large datasets, identify patterns, and make predictions, helping organizations make informed decisions.

- **Healthcare**: AI algorithms analyze patient data, medical records, and research findings to assist doctors in diagnosing diseases, predicting patient outcomes, and developing personalized treatment plans. This leads to more accurate diagnoses, better patient care, and improved health outcomes.

- **Finance**: AI models predict market trends, assess investment risks, and detect fraudulent activities. Financial institutions use these insights to make strategic decisions, optimize portfolios, and enhance security measures.

- **Supply Chain Management**: AI optimizes supply chain operations by forecasting demand, managing inventory, and identifying inefficiencies. This leads to cost savings, improved resource allocation, and reduced waste.

Personalization

AI enables highly personalized experiences in various applications, enhancing user satisfaction and engagement.

- **Retail**: E-commerce platforms use AI to analyze customer behavior and preferences, offering personalized product recommendations and targeted marketing campaigns. This not only boosts sales but also enhances the shopping experience.

- **Entertainment**: Streaming services like Netflix and Spotify use AI to recommend content based on users' viewing and listening habits. This personalization keeps users engaged and encourages them to explore new content.

- **Education**: AI-powered educational platforms provide personalized learning experiences by adapting to individual learning styles and paces. This helps students achieve better outcomes and makes learning more enjoyable.

Revolutionizing Healthcare

AI is transforming healthcare by improving diagnostics, enhancing patient care, and accelerating medical research.

- **Medical Imaging**: AI algorithms analyze medical images, such as X-rays, MRIs, and CT scans, to detect abnormalities and diagnose diseases with high accuracy. This assists radiologists in making faster and more accurate diagnoses.

- **Drug Discovery**: AI accelerates the drug discovery process by analyzing vast amounts of chemical and biological data to identify potential drug candidates. This reduces the time and cost involved in bringing new drugs to market.

- **Predictive Analytics**: AI analyzes patient data to predict disease outbreaks, identify high-risk patients, and recommend preventive measures. This proactive approach improves public health outcomes and reduces healthcare costs.

Enhancing Safety and Security

AI enhances safety and security in various domains, from cybersecurity to physical security.

- **Cybersecurity**: AI systems detect and respond to cyber threats in real time by analyzing network traffic, identifying anomalies, and predicting potential attacks. This helps organizations protect their sensitive data and maintain the integrity of their systems.

- **Surveillance**: AI-powered surveillance systems monitor public spaces, detect suspicious activities, and alert authorities to potential threats. This enhances public safety and aids in crime prevention.

- **Autonomous Vehicles**: AI technology in self-driving cars improves road safety by reducing human error, optimizing traffic flow, and preventing accidents. Autonomous vehicles use AI to navigate, avoid obstacles, and make real-time driving decisions.

Driving Innovation

AI drives innovation by enabling the development of new applications, products, and services that were previously unimaginable.

- **Smart Cities**: AI technologies optimize urban infrastructure, including traffic management, energy consumption, and waste management. This leads to more sustainable and efficient cities.

- **Robotics**: AI-powered robots perform complex tasks in various industries, from manufacturing and healthcare to agriculture and logistics. These robots enhance productivity, reduce labor costs, and improve safety.

- **Creative Industries**: AI is used in creative industries to generate art, music, and literature. AI algorithms can compose music, create visual art, and even write stories, opening up new possibilities for artistic expression.

Addressing Global Challenges

AI has the potential to address some of the world's most pressing challenges, from climate change to food security.

- **Climate Change**: AI analyzes climate data to predict weather patterns, model the impacts of environmental policies, and optimize energy use. This helps in mitigating the effects of climate change and developing sustainable solutions.

- **Agriculture**: AI-powered technologies monitor crop health, optimize irrigation, and predict yield. This improves agricultural productivity, reduces resource use, and ensures food security.

- **Disaster Response**: AI systems analyze data from natural disasters, such as earthquakes and hurricanes, to predict their impacts and coordinate response efforts. This enhances disaster preparedness and reduces the loss of life and property.

Enhancing Human Capabilities

AI enhances human capabilities by augmenting our abilities and enabling us to achieve more.

- **Assistive Technologies**: AI-powered assistive technologies, such as speech recognition software and smart prosthetics, help individuals with disabilities live more independently and participate fully in society.

- **Augmented Intelligence**: AI systems assist professionals in various fields, from medicine to engineering, by providing data-driven insights and recommendations. This enhances decision-making and problem-solving capabilities.

- **Personal Productivity**: AI-powered tools, such as virtual assistants and smart home devices, help individuals manage their daily tasks, stay organized, and improve their productivity.

Ethical and Responsible Use of AI

While AI offers numerous benefits, it also raises ethical and societal concerns that must be addressed to ensure its responsible use.

- **Bias and Fairness**: AI systems can perpetuate and amplify biases present in the training data. Ensuring fairness and preventing discrimination requires developing unbiased algorithms, using diverse datasets, and continuously monitoring AI systems for bias.

- **Privacy and Security**: AI systems often require access to vast amounts of personal data, raising concerns about privacy and data security. Implementing robust data protection measures and ensuring transparency in data collection and use are essential to address these concerns.

- **Job Displacement**: The automation of tasks by AI can lead to job displacement in certain sectors. Addressing this issue requires investing in education and training programs to help workers transition to new roles and ensuring that the benefits of AI are distributed equitably.

- **Accountability and Transparency**: AI systems should be designed and deployed in a transparent manner, with clear accountability for their actions and decisions. This includes providing explanations for AI-driven decisions and establishing mechanisms for addressing grievances and disputes.

Artificial Intelligence is a powerful tool that has the potential to transform industries, enhance human capabilities, and address global challenges. Its importance lies in its ability to automate tasks, improve decision-making, personalize experiences, revolutionize healthcare, enhance safety and security, drive innovation, and tackle pressing issues such as climate change and food security.

However, the responsible and ethical use of AI is crucial to ensure that its benefits are realized while mitigating potential risks. By addressing concerns related to bias, privacy, job displacement, and accountability, we can harness the full potential of AI to create a better future for all.

Chapter 4: Advantages and Disadvantages of AI

Introduction

As Artificial Intelligence (AI) continues to evolve, it brings with it a host of advantages that can transform various aspects of our lives. However, it also presents certain disadvantages and challenges that need to be carefully managed. This chapter provides a comprehensive overview of the pros and cons of AI, examining how it can benefit society while also addressing the potential drawbacks and ethical concerns.

Advantages of AI

Efficiency and Productivity
One of the most significant advantages of AI is its ability to enhance efficiency and productivity. AI systems can perform repetitive and time-consuming tasks quickly and accurately, freeing up human workers to focus on more complex and creative activities.

- **Automation**: AI can automate routine tasks such as data entry, scheduling, and customer service, leading to increased productivity and reduced operational costs.

- **Precision and Accuracy**: AI systems can perform tasks with a high degree of accuracy, reducing the likelihood of human error. This is particularly valuable in fields such as manufacturing, healthcare, and finance.

- **24/7 Availability**: Unlike humans, AI systems can operate continuously without breaks, providing round-the-clock support and services.

Enhanced Decision Making

AI enhances decision-making processes by providing data-driven insights and recommendations. This leads to better outcomes and more informed decisions.

- **Data Analysis**: AI can analyze vast amounts of data quickly, identifying patterns, trends, and correlations that may not be apparent to humans. This enables organizations to make more informed decisions based on data.

- **Predictive Analytics**: AI algorithms can predict future trends and outcomes based on historical data. This is valuable in fields such as finance, healthcare, and marketing, where accurate predictions can lead to better decision-making.

- **Real-Time Insights**: AI systems can provide real-time insights and recommendations, enabling organizations to respond quickly to changing conditions and make timely decisions.

Personalization

AI enables highly personalized experiences in various applications, enhancing user satisfaction and engagement.

- **Retail**: AI-powered recommendation systems analyze customer behavior and preferences to offer personalized product recommendations. This improves the shopping experience and increases sales.

- **Entertainment**: Streaming services use AI to recommend movies, TV shows, and music based on users' viewing and listening habits. This keeps users engaged and encourages them to explore new content.

- **Education**: AI-powered educational platforms provide personalized learning experiences by adapting to individual learning styles and paces. This helps students achieve better outcomes and makes learning more enjoyable.

Healthcare Advancements

AI is revolutionizing healthcare by improving diagnostics,enhancing patient care, and accelerating medical research.

- **Medical Imaging**: AI algorithms analyze medical images, such as X-rays, MRIs, and CT scans, to detect abnormalities and diagnose diseases with high accuracy. This assists radiologists in making faster and more accurate diagnoses.

- **Drug Discovery**: AI accelerates the drug discovery process by analyzing vast amounts of chemical and biological data to identify potential drug candidates. This reduces the time and cost involved in bringing new drugs to market.

- **Predictive Analytics**: AI analyzes patient data to predict disease outbreaks, identify high-risk patients, and recommend preventive measures. This proactive approach improves public health outcomes and reduces healthcare costs.

Enhancing Safety and Security

AI enhances safety and security in various domains, from cybersecurity to physical security.

- **Cybersecurity**: AI systems detect and respond to cyber threats in real time by analyzing network traffic, identifying anomalies, and predicting potential attacks. This helps organizations protect their sensitive data and maintain the integrity of their systems.

- **Surveillance**: AI-powered surveillance systems monitor public spaces, detect suspicious activities, and alert authorities to potential threats. This enhances public safety and aids in crime prevention.

- **Autonomous Vehicles**: AI technology in self-driving cars improves road safety by reducing human error, optimizing traffic flow, and preventing accidents. Autonomous vehicles use AI to navigate, avoid obstacles, and make real-time driving decisions.

Driving Innovation

AI drives innovation by enabling the development of new applications, products, and services that were previously unimaginable.

- **Smart Cities**: AI technologies optimize urban infrastructure, including traffic management, energy consumption, and waste management. This leads to more sustainable and efficient cities.

- **Robotics**: AI-powered robots perform complex tasks in various industries, from manufacturing and healthcare to agriculture and logistics. These robots enhance productivity, reduce labor costs, and improve safety.

- **Creative Industries**: AI is used in creative industries to generate art, music, and literature. AI algorithms can compose music, create visual art, and even write stories, opening up new possibilities for artistic expression.

Addressing Global Challenges

AI has the potential to address some of the world's most pressing challenges, from climate change to food security.

- **Climate Change**: AI analyzes climate data to predict weather patterns, model the impacts of environmental policies, and optimize energy use. This helps in mitigating the effects of climate change and developing sustainable solutions.
- **Agriculture**: AI-powered technologies monitor crop health, optimize irrigation, and predict yield. This improves agricultural productivity, reduces resource use, and ensures food security.
- **Disaster Response**: AI systems analyze data from natural disasters, such as earthquakes and hurricanes, to predict their impacts and coordinate response efforts. This enhances disaster preparedness and reduces the loss of life and property.

Disadvantages of AI

While AI offers numerous benefits, it also presents certain disadvantages and challenges that must be carefully managed.

Job Displacement
One of the most significant concerns about AI is its potential to displace jobs, particularly in sectors that rely heavily on routine and repetitive tasks.

- **Automation:** As AI systems automate tasks previously performed by humans, there is a risk of job loss in industries such as manufacturing, customer service, and data entry.

- **Skill Mismatch:** Workers displaced by AI may lack the skills needed for new roles created by AI-driven industries. This can lead to unemployment and economic inequality if adequate retraining and upskilling programs are not provided.

- **Economic Disruption:** Widespread job displacement could lead to economic disruption, affecting not only individuals but also communities and entire industries.

High Costs

Developing and maintaining AI systems can be expensive, posing a barrier to entry for smaller organizations and developing countries.

- **Development Costs**: Building AI systems requires significant investment in research, data collection, and algorithm development. This can be prohibitively expensive for smaller organizations and startups.

- **Computational Resources**: AI systems require substantial computational power, which can be costly. High-performance hardware, such as GPUs and TPUs, is necessary to train and run complex AI models.

- **Maintenance and Updates**: AI systems require ongoing maintenance and updates to ensure they continue to perform effectively and adapt to new data and changing conditions. This adds to the overall cost of AI implementation.

Bias and Fairness

AI systems can perpetuate and amplify biases present in the training data, leading to unfair and discriminatory outcomes.

- **Biased Data**: AI systems learn from the data they are trained on. If this data contains biases, the AI system may learn and replicate these biases, leading to unfair treatment of certain groups.

- **Algorithmic Bias**: Even if the training data is unbiased, the design of the AI algorithms themselves can introduce bias. Ensuring fairness requires careful design, testing, and evaluation of AI systems.

- **Impact on Marginalized Groups**: Biased AI systems can disproportionately impact marginalized and vulnerable groups, exacerbating existing inequalities and injustices.

Security Risks

AI systems can be vulnerable to attacks and misuse, posing significant security risks.

- **Adversarial Attacks**: AI systems can be tricked by adversarial examples, where input data is intentionally manipulated to deceive the AI. This can lead to incorrect predictions or decisions, with potentially serious consequences.

- **Data Breaches**: AI systems often require access to large amounts of sensitive data, making them attractive targets for cyberattacks. Ensuring the security of this data is critical to prevent breaches and protect privacy.

- **Malicious Use**: AI technology can be used for malicious purposes, such as creating deepfakes, conducting cyberattacks, or developing autonomous weapons. Preventing the misuse of AI is a major challenge that requires robust regulations and oversight.

Dependence on Technology

Over-reliance on AI and technology can lead to a loss of human skills and decision-making abilities.

- **Skill Degradation**: As AI systems take over more tasks, there is a risk that humans may lose the skills required to perform these tasks. This can lead to a loss of expertise and a diminished ability to function without AI.

- **Decision-Making**: Relying too heavily on AI for decision-making can lead to a loss of critical thinking and problem-solving skills. It is important to maintain a balance between human judgment and AI-driven insights.

- **Technological Dependence**: Increased dependence on AI and technology can make societies vulnerable to technological failures or disruptions. Ensuring resilience and maintaining backup systems are crucial to mitigate these risks.

Ethical Considerations

The deployment of AI raises several ethical concerns that must be addressed to ensure its responsible use.

Privacy and Surveillance

AI systems often require access to vast amounts of personal data, raising concerns about privacy and surveillance.

- **Data Collection**: The collection of personal data by AI systems can infringe on individuals' privacy rights. Ensuring transparency and obtaining informed consent are essential to address these concerns.

- **Surveillance**: AI-powered surveillance systems can be used for mass monitoring and tracking of individuals, raising concerns about civil liberties and the potential for abuse by authorities.

- **Data Security**: Protecting the security of personal data is crucial to prevent breaches and misuse. Robust data protection measures must be implemented to safeguard individuals' privacy.

Accountability and Transparency

Ensuring accountability and transparency in AI systems is essential to build trust and address ethical concerns.

- **Explainability**: Many AI systems operate as "black boxes," making it difficult to understand how they arrive at their decisions. Improving the explainability of AI systems is crucial to ensure accountability and trust.

- **Responsibility**: Establishing clear lines of responsibility for AI-driven decisions is essential to address grievances and disputes. This includes defining who is accountable when AI systems make errors or cause harm.

- **Regulation**: Developing and enforcing regulations for the ethical use of AI is crucial to prevent misuse and ensure that AI systems are developed and deployed responsibly.

Societal Impact

The widespread adoption of AI has the potential to reshape society in significant ways, raising important ethical considerations.

- **Economic Inequality**: The benefits of AI may not be distributed equally, potentially exacerbating economic inequality. Ensuring that the benefits of AI are shared broadly and equitably is essential to address this concern.

- **Human-AI Interaction**: The increasing interaction between humans and AI systems raises questions about the nature of relationships and trust. Ensuring that AI systems are designed to complement human abilities and enhance human well-being is crucial.

- **Cultural and Social Norms**: The deployment of AI can impact cultural and social norms in various ways. Ensuring that AI systems are developed and deployed in a manner that respects and preserves cultural diversity and social values is important.

Chapter 5: Types of AI

Introduction

Artificial Intelligence (AI) encompasses a broad range of technologies and approaches, each with its unique characteristics and capabilities. Understanding the different types of AI is essential to grasp their diverse applications and the scope of their potential impact. This chapter will explore the various types of AI, from simple reactive machines to advanced, self-aware systems, providing a comprehensive overview of their characteristics, capabilities, and applications.

Categories of AI Based on Capabilities

AI can be categorized into different types based on their capabilities, ranging from narrow AI systems designed for specific tasks to hypothetical advanced systems with human-like cognitive abilities.

Narrow AI (Weak AI)

Narrow AI, also known as Weak AI, is designed and trained to perform a specific task or a set of related tasks. These systems excel in their designated areas but lack the ability to generalize their knowledge to other domains.

Characteristics of Narrow AI:

- **Task-Specific**: Narrow AI is built to perform a particular task, such as language translation, image recognition, or playing a specific game.

- **High Accuracy**: These systems can achieve high accuracy and efficiency in their specialized tasks.

- **No Generalization**: Narrow AI cannot apply its knowledge or skills to tasks outside its specific domain.

Examples of Narrow AI:

- **Virtual Assistants**: AI-powered virtual assistants like Siri, Alexa, and Google Assistant help with tasks such as setting reminders, answering questions, and controlling smart home devices.

- **Recommendation Systems**: Platforms like Netflix, Amazon, and Spotify use AI to recommend movies, products, and music based on user preferences.

- **Image Recognition** Software: AI algorithms used in medical diagnostics to detect diseases from medical images, or in security systems to identify faces in surveillance footage.

General AI (Strong AI)

General AI, also known as Strong AI or Artificial General Intelligence (AGI), refers to systems that possess the ability to understand, learn, and apply knowledge across a wide range of tasks at a level comparable to human intelligence. Unlike Narrow AI, AGI systems can generalize their knowledge and skills to different domains.

Characteristics of General AI:
- **Human-Like Intelligence**: AGI systems can perform any intellectual task that a human can do.

- **Adaptability**: These systems can adapt to new situations and learn from diverse experiences.

- **Generalization**: AGI can apply knowledge from one domain to solve problems in another domain.

Current Status of General AI:
- AGI remains a theoretical concept and has not yet been achieved. Researchers are still exploring the fundamental principles required to develop such systems.

Superintelligent AI

Superintelligent AI refers to hypothetical systems that surpass human intelligence across all domains. These systems would not only perform intellectual tasks at a superhuman level but also possess superior cognitive abilities.

Characteristics of Superintelligent AI:

- **Superior Cognitive Abilities**: Superintelligent AI would outperform human intelligence in all areas, including problem-solving, creativity, and emotional intelligence.

- **Self-Improving**: These systems would have the ability to improve their own algorithms and capabilities autonomously.

- **Ethical and Existential Concerns**: The development of superintelligent AI raises significant ethical and existential concerns, including the potential for unintended consequences and the need for robust control mechanisms.

Current Status of Superintelligent AI:

- Superintelligent AI remains a theoretical concept and is the subject of much debate and speculation among researchers and ethicists.

Categories of AI Based on Functionality

AI systems can also be categorized based on their functionality and the complexity of the tasks they can perform. This classification includes reactive machines, limited memory systems, theory of mind, and self-aware AI.

Reactive Machines

Reactive machines are the simplest type of AI systems. They can respond to specific inputs with pre-programmed outputs but have no memory or ability to learn from past experiences.

Characteristics of Reactive Machines:

- **No Memory**: These systems do not store past experiences or learn from them.

- **Task-Specific**: Reactive machines are designed to perform specific tasks based on predefined rules.

- **Real-Time Response**: They can respond to inputs in real-time but cannot adapt or improve over time.

Examples of Reactive Machines:

- **Deep Blue**: IBM's chess-playing computer, Deep Blue, is a classic example of a reactive machine. It could analyze the current state of a chess game and make decisions based on predefined rules and strategies.

- **Spam Filters**: Basic spam filters that identify and block unwanted emails based on predefined criteria are another example of reactive machines.

Limited Memory

Limited memory AI systems have the capability to store and use past experiences to inform future decisions. These systems can learn from historical data and improve their performance over time.

Characteristics of Limited Memory AI:

- **Memory Utilization**: These systems can store and use past data to improve decision-making.

- **Learning Ability**: Limited memory AI can learn from historical data and adapt to new information.

- **Application**-Specific: While they can learn and adapt, these systems are still designed for specific tasks.

Examples of Limited Memory AI:
- **Self-Driving Cars**: Autonomous vehicles use limited memory AI to learn from past driving experiences, traffic patterns, and road conditions to make real-time driving decisions.
- **Personalized Recommendations**: AI systems that provide personalized recommendations based on users' past behaviors and preferences, such as e-commerce recommendations, utilize limited memory AI.

Theory of Mind

Theory of mind AI systems represent a more advanced stage of AI development, where machines can understand human emotions, beliefs, and intentions. These systems are capable of social interactions and can engage in meaningful conversations with humans.

Characteristics of Theory of Mind AI:

- **Emotional Intelligence**: These systems can recognize and respond to human emotions and intentions.

- **Social Interaction**: Theory of mind AI can engage in complex social interactions and understand the context of conversations.

- **Human-Like Understanding**: These systems possess a deeper understanding of human behavior and thought processes.

Current Status of Theory of Mind AI:
- Theory of mind AI is still in the early stages of research and development. While there have been advancements in natural language processing and emotion recognition, fully functional theory of mind AI systems have not yet been realized.

Self-Aware AI

Self-aware AI represents the pinnacle of AI development, where machines possess self-awareness and consciousness. These systems would have a sense of self and the ability to understand their own existence.

Characteristics of Self-Aware AI:

- **Consciousness**: Self-aware AI systems have a sense of self and consciousness.

- **Self-Improvement**: These systems can understand their own limitations and improve their capabilities autonomously.

- **Ethical and Existential Implications**: The development of self-aware AI raises profound ethical and existential questions, including the nature of consciousness and the rights of AI entities.

Current Status of Self-Aware AI:

- Self-aware AI remains a speculative concept and is the subject of ongoing philosophical and scientific debate. Researchers have not yet developed technologies that confer self-awareness or consciousness to machines.

AI Techniques and Approaches

Different techniques and approaches are used to develop AI systems, each with its unique strengths and applications. Some of the most common techniques include machine learning, deep learning, natural language processing, and computer vision.

Machine Learning

Machine learning is a subset of AI that involves training algorithms to learn from data and make predictions or decisions without being explicitly programmed. There are three main types of machine learning:

Supervised Learning: In supervised learning, the AI system is trained on a labeled dataset, where each input comes with an associated output. The goal is to learn a mapping from inputs to outputs.

- **Examples**: Spam detection, image classification, and predictive analytics.

Unsupervised Learning: In unsupervised learning, the AI system is given unlabeled data and must find patterns or structures within the data.

- **Examples**: Customer segmentation, anomaly detection, and clustering.

Reinforcement Learning: In reinforcement learning, the AI system learns by interacting with its environment and receiving feedback in the form of rewards or penalties. The goal is to learn a policy that maximizes cumulative rewards.

- **Examples**: Game playing (e.g., AlphaGo), robotic control, and autonomous navigation.

Deep Learning

Deep learning is a specialized subset of machine learning that uses neural networks with many layers (hence "deep") to model complex patterns in data. Neural networks are inspired by the structure and function of the human brain.

Key Concepts in Deep Learning:

- **Neural Networks**: Composed of layers of interconnected nodes (neurons), where each node processes input and passes the output to the next layer.

- **Training Neural Networks**: Involves adjusting the weights of the connections between nodes to minimize the error between the predicted output and the actual output.

- **Activation Functions**: Non-linear functions applied at each node to introduce non-linearity into the network, allowing it to model complex relationships.

- **Optimization Algorithms**: Methods used to minimize the error during training, such as gradient descent and its variants (e.g., stochastic gradient descent, Adam).

Applications of Deep Learning:

- **Image and Speech Recognition**: Deep learning models, such as convolutional neural networks (CNNs) and recurrent neural networks (RNNs), are used for tasks like image classification, object detection, and speech recognition.

- **Natural Language Processing (NLP)**: Deep learning techniques, such as transformers, are used for tasks like language translation, sentiment analysis, and text generation.

Natural Language Processing (NLP)

Natural Language Processing (NLP) is a field of AI that focuses on the interaction between computers and human languages. NLP enables machines to understand, interpret, and generate human language.

Key Techniques in NLP:
- **Tokenization**: Breaking down text into smaller units, such as words or sentences.

- **Part-of-Speech Tagging**: Identifying the grammatical parts of speech (e.g., nouns, verbs) in a text.

- **Named Entity Recognition (NER)**: Identifying and classifying entities (e.g., names, dates, locations) within a text.

- **Sentiment Analysis**: Determining the sentiment or emotional tone of a piece of text.

- **Language Modeling**: Predicting the next word or sequence of words in a sentence.

-

Applications of NLP:

- **Chatbots and Virtual Assistants**: NLP powers the language understanding and generation capabilities of chatbots and virtual assistants, enabling them to interact with users in natural language.

- **Machine Translation**: Systems like Google Translate use NLP to translate text from one language to another.

- **Text Summarization**: NLP techniques are used to automatically generate concise summaries of long documents.

Computer Vision

Computer vision is a field of AI that enables machines to interpret and understand visual information from the world, such as images and videos.

Key Techniques in Computer Vision:

- **Image Classification**: Assigning labels to images based on their content (e.g., recognizing objects in an image).

- **Object Detection**: Identifying and locating objects within an image.

- **Image Segmentation**: Dividing an image into segments or regions for analysis.

- **Facial Recognition**: Identifying and verifying individuals based on their facial features.

Applications of Computer Vision:

- **Medical Imaging**: AI algorithms analyze medical images to detect diseases and assist in diagnosis.

- **Autonomous Vehicles**: Self-driving cars use computer vision to perceive their environment and make driving decisions.

- **Security and Surveillance**: AI-powered surveillance systems use computer vision to monitor public spaces and detect suspicious activities.

Emerging AI Technologies

AI continues to evolve, with new technologies and approaches emerging that push the boundaries of what is possible.

Generative Adversarial Networks (GANs)

Generative Adversarial Networks (GANs) are a type of AI that can generate new content, such as images, music, and text, by pitting two neural networks against each other: the generator and the discriminator.

How GANs Work:

- **Generator**: Creates fake data that is intended to be indistinguishable from real data.

- **Discriminator**: Evaluates the authenticity of the data, distinguishing between real and fake data.

- **Training**: The generator and discriminator are trained together, with the generator improving its ability to create realistic data, and the discriminator improving its ability to detect fakes.

Applications of GANs:

- **Image Generation**: GANs can generate realistic images of faces, landscapes, and objects.

- **Art and Design**: Artists and designers use GANs to create unique and innovative artwork.

- **Data Augmentation**: GANs generate synthetic data to augment training datasets, improving the performance of AI models.

Transfer Learning

Transfer learning is an approach in AI where a model trained on one task is adapted for use on a related task. This technique leverages the knowledge gained from the initial task to improve performance on the new task.

How Transfer Learning Works:

- **Pre-trained Model**: A model is initially trained on a large dataset for a general task.
- **Fine-Tuning**: The pre-trained model is fine-tuned on a smaller, task-specific dataset to adapt it for the new task.

Applications of Transfer Learning:

- **Image Recognition**: Pre-trained models on large image datasets (e.g., ImageNet) are fine-tuned for specific image recognition tasks.

- **NLP**: Pre-trained language models, such as BERT and GPT, are fine-tuned for specific NLP tasks like sentiment analysis or question answering.

Reinforcement Learning (RL)

Reinforcement learning is a type of machine learning where an agent learns to make decisions by interacting with its environment and receiving rewards or penalties.

How Reinforcement Learning Works:

- **Agent**: The decision-making entity that interacts with the environment.

- **Environment**: The setting in which the agent operates and takes actions.

- **Policy**: The strategy that the agent uses to decide which actions to take.

- **Reward Signal**: Feedback from the environment that indicates the success or failure of the agent's actions.

Applications of Reinforcement Learning:

- **Game Playing**: RL algorithms, such as AlphaGo, learn to play and master complex games by receiving rewards for successful moves.

- **Robotics**: RL is used to train robots to perform tasks like grasping objects and navigating environments.

- **Autonomous Vehicles**: RL algorithms help self-driving cars learn to make driving decisions in dynamic environments.

Specialized AI Systems

AI systems are often specialized for specific applications, each with unique requirements and challenges.

Expert Systems

Expert systems are AI programs that emulate the decision-making abilities of a human expert in a specific domain. These systems use a knowledge base of facts and rules to solve complex problems.

Characteristics of Expert Systems:

- **Knowledge Base**: A repository of domain-specific knowledge, including facts and rules.

- **Inference Engine**: The component that applies logical rules to the knowledge base to derive conclusions and make decisions.

- **User Interface**: The interface through which users interact with the expert system.

Applications of Expert Systems:

- **Medical Diagnosis**: Expert systems assist doctors in diagnosing diseases by analyzing symptoms and medical history.

- **Legal Advice**: These systems provide legal advice based on a knowledge base of laws and regulations.

- **Financial Planning**: Expert systems offer financial planning and investment advice based on economic data and market trends.

Robotics

Robotics is an interdisciplinary field that combines AI with mechanical engineering and computer science to design and build robots that can perform tasks autonomously or semi-autonomously.

Key Components of Robotics:

- **Sensors**: Devices that gather information about the robot's environment (e.g., cameras, LIDAR, touch sensors).

- **Actuators**: Components that enable the robot to move and interact with its environment (e.g., motors, grippers).

- **Control Systems**: Algorithms and software that control the robot's actions and decision-making processes.

Applications of Robotics:

- **Manufacturing**: Industrial robots perform tasks such as assembly, welding, and painting in manufacturing plants.

- **Healthcare**: Robots assist in surgeries, provide rehabilitation therapy, and care for elderly patients.

- **Exploration**: Robots explore extreme environments, such as deep oceans and outer space, where human presence is challenging.

Chapter 6: Examples of AI Technologies and Its Uses

Introduction

Artificial Intelligence (AI) is no longer a futuristic concept confined to the realms of science fiction. Today, AI technologies are integrated into various aspects of our daily lives and are transforming industries across the globe. This chapter provides a detailed exploration of the practical applications of AI, showcasing real-world examples of how AI is being used today to drive innovation, improve efficiency, and enhance human capabilities.

AI in Healthcare

AI is revolutionizing the healthcare industry by enhancing diagnostic accuracy, personalizing treatment plans, and accelerating medical research. Here are some prominent examples of AI applications in healthcare:

Medical Imaging and Diagnostics

AI algorithms are used to analyze medical images such as X-rays, MRIs, and CT scans to detect abnormalities and diagnose diseases.

Examples:

- **Google DeepMind**: DeepMind's AI system can diagnose over 50 eye diseases with accuracy comparable to that of expert ophthalmologists by analyzing retinal scans.

- **Aidoc**: Aidoc's AI-powered radiology software assists radiologists by identifying critical findings in medical images, such as brain hemorrhages and lung nodules.

Personalized Medicine

AI helps in developing personalized treatment plans based on individual patient data, including genetic information, lifestyle factors, and medical history.

Examples:

- **IBM Watson for Oncology**: Watson analyzes patient data and medical literature to recommend personalized cancer treatment plans, aiding oncologists in making informed decisions.

- **Tempus**: Tempus uses AI to analyze clinical and molecular data to provide personalized insights for cancer treatment, helping doctors tailor therapies to individual patients.

Drug Discovery

AI accelerates the drug discovery process by analyzing vast amounts of chemical and biological data to identify potential drug candidates.

Examples:

- **Insilico Medicine**: Insilico Medicine uses AI to discover new drug compounds and predict their efficacy, significantly reducing the time and cost of drug development.

- **Atomwise**: **Atomwise's** AI platform uses deep learning to predict the binding affinity of small molecules to protein targets, aiding in the discovery of new therapeutics.

AI in Finance

The financial industry leverages AI to improve decision-making, enhance security, and provide personalized services to customers. Here are some key applications of AI in finance:

Fraud Detection

AI systems analyze transaction data to detect fraudulent activities in real time, protecting customers and financial institutions from financial losses.

Examples:

- **Visa**: Visa uses AI to monitor transactions and detect fraudulent patterns, preventing billions of dollars in fraudulent activities each year.

- **Mastercard**: **Mastercard's** AI-powered fraud detection system analyzes over 75 billion transactions annually to identify and block suspicious transactions.

Algorithmic Trading

AI algorithms analyze market data and execute trades at high speeds, optimizing investment strategies and maximizing returns.

Examples:

- **Renaissance Technologies**: Renaissance Technologies, a hedge fund, uses AI and quantitative models to execute algorithmic trades and achieve significant returns on investments. Their AI-driven strategies analyze vast amounts of market data to identify profitable trading opportunities.

- **Kensho Technologies**: Kensho's AI-powered analytics platform helps financial institutions and traders analyze market movements, predict trends, and execute trades based on data-driven insights.

Personalized Financial Services

AI enables financial institutions to offer personalized services and recommendations to their customers, enhancing the overall customer experience.

Examples:
- **Betterment**: Betterment uses AI to provide personalized investment advice and automated portfolio management, helping users achieve their financial goals.

- **Cleo**: Cleo is an AI-powered financial assistant that helps users manage their finances by providing insights into spending habits, budgeting tips, and savings recommendations.

AI in Retail

The retail industry leverages AI to enhance customer experiences, optimize operations, and improve supply chain management. Here are some key applications of AI in retail:

Personalized Shopping Experiences

AI analyzes customer data to offer personalized product recommendations and targeted marketing campaigns, increasing customer satisfaction and sales.

Examples:

- **Amazon**: Amazon uses AI to recommend products based on customers' browsing and purchasing history, significantly boosting sales and customer retention.

- **Sephora**: Sephora's AI-powered virtual assistant helps customers find products that match their preferences and skin tones, offering personalized beauty recommendations.

Inventory Management

AI optimizes inventory management by predicting demand, reducing overstock and stockouts, and improving supply chain efficiency.

Examples:

- **Walmart**: Walmart uses AI to forecast demand, manage inventory levels, and optimize supply chain operations, ensuring that products are always available when customers need them.

- **Zara**: Zara employs AI to analyze sales data and predict fashion trends, allowing the company to manage inventory efficiently and respond quickly to changing customer preferences.

Customer Service

AI-powered chatbots and virtual assistants provide instant customer support, resolving issues and answering queries efficiently.

Examples:
- **H&M**: H&M uses AI chatbots to assist customers with product inquiries, order tracking, and returns, enhancing the overall shopping experience.

- **Lowe's**: Lowe's AI-powered virtual assistant helps customers find products, check inventory, and answer questions about home improvement projects.

AI in Transportation

The transportation industry leverages AI to improve safety, efficiency, and sustainability. Here are some prominent examples of AI applications in transportation:

Autonomous Vehicles

AI powers self-driving cars, enabling them to navigate roads, avoid obstacles, and make real-time driving decisions.

Examples:

- **Tesla**: Tesla's Autopilot system uses AI to enable semi-autonomous driving, with features such as lane-keeping, adaptive cruise control, and automated parking.

- **Waymo**: Waymo's fully autonomous vehicles use AI to navigate complex urban environments, providing safe and efficient transportation without human intervention.

Traffic Management

AI optimizes traffic flow and reduces congestion by analyzing real-time traffic data and adjusting traffic signals accordingly.

Examples:

- **Surtrac**: Surtrac's AI-powered traffic management system optimizes traffic signal timings based on real-time traffic conditions, reducing congestion and improving travel times in cities.

- **IBM Watson**: IBM Watson's AI solutions help cities analyze traffic patterns, predict congestion, and optimize traffic management to improve overall transportation efficiency.

Fleet Management

AI improves fleet management by optimizing routes, predicting maintenance needs, and reducing operational costs.

Examples:
- **UPS**: UPS uses AI to optimize delivery routes, reducing fuel consumption and improving delivery efficiency. Their ORION (On-Road Integrated Optimization and Navigation) system analyzes data from millions of deliveries to find the most efficient routes.

- **Geotab**: Geotab's AI-powered fleet management solutions help companies monitor vehicle performance, predict maintenance needs, and optimize fleet operations.

AI in Manufacturing

The manufacturing industry leverages AI to enhance production processes, improve quality control, and increase efficiency. Here are some key applications of AI in manufacturing:

Predictive Maintenance

AI predicts equipment failures before they occur, allowing for proactive maintenance and reducing downtime.

Examples:

- **Siemens**: Siemens uses AI to monitor equipment health and predict maintenance needs, preventing unexpected failures and optimizing maintenance schedules.

- **GE Digital**: GE Digital's AI-powered Predix platform analyzes data from industrial equipment to predict failures and recommend maintenance actions, improving equipment reliability and performance.

Quality Control

AI enhances quality control by inspecting products for defects and ensuring that they meet quality standards.

Examples:

- **Fanuc**: Fanuc's AI-powered robots inspect parts and products for defects, ensuring high quality and reducing waste in manufacturing processes.

- **Landing.ai**: Landing.ai's computer vision technology detects defects in manufacturing processes with high accuracy, helping manufacturers improve product quality and reduce production costs.

Supply Chain Optimization

AI optimizes supply chain operations by predicting demand, managing inventory, and improving logistics.

Examples:
- **Flexport**: Flexport uses AI to optimize global supply chain operations, providing real-time visibility into shipments and predicting potential disruptions.

- **ClearMetal**: ClearMetal's AI-powered platform analyzes supply chain data to improve demand forecasting, inventory management, and logistics planning.

AI in Education

The education sector leverages AI to provide personalized learning experiences, automate administrative tasks, and enhance student engagement. Here are some key applications of AI in education:

Personalized Learning

AI tailors educational content and learning experiences to individual students' needs, preferences, and learning styles.

Examples:

- **Knewton**: Knewton's AI-powered adaptive learning platform personalizes educational content based on students' strengths and weaknesses, helping them achieve better learning outcomes.

-

- **DreamBox**: DreamBox uses AI to provide personalized math instruction for K-8 students, adapting lessons to each student's skill level and learning pace.

Intelligent Tutoring Systems

AI-powered tutoring systems provide personalized assistance and feedback to students, enhancing their understanding of complex subjects.

Examples:

- **Carnegie Learning**: Carnegie Learning's AI-powered tutoring systems provide personalized math instruction and feedback, helping students improve their math skills and performance.

- **Socratic**: Socratic, acquired by Google, uses AI to provide students with step-by-step solutions and explanations for homework questions, enhancing their understanding of various subjects.

Administrative Automation

AI automates administrative tasks such as grading, scheduling, and student record management, reducing the workload for educators and administrative staff.

Examples:
- **GradeScope**: GradeScope uses AI to automate grading for assignments and exams, providing instant feedback to students and saving time for educators.

- **Coursera**: Coursera's AI-powered platform automates course recommendations, progress tracking, and certification management, improving the efficiency of online education.

AI in Agriculture

The agriculture industry leverages AI to improve crop yields, optimize resource use, and enhance sustainability. Here are some key applications of AI in agriculture:

Precision Farming

AI-powered precision farming technologies monitor and manage crops, optimizing resource use and improving yields.

Examples:

- **John Deere**: John Deere's AI-powered equipment uses sensors and machine learning to optimize planting, irrigation, and fertilization, improving crop yields and reducing resource use.

- **FarmWise**: FarmWise's AI-powered robots perform tasks such as weeding and harvesting with high precision, reducing labor costs and improving efficiency in farming operations.

Crop Monitoring

AI systems monitor crop health and detect diseases, enabling timely interventions and reducing crop losses.

Examples:

- **Sentera**: Sentera's AI-powered drones and sensors monitor crop health, providing farmers with real-time data and insights to manage their crops effectively.

- **Taranis**: Taranis uses AI to analyze high-resolution aerial imagery, detecting early signs of crop diseases and pests, allowing farmers to take proactive measures.

Yield Prediction

AI predicts crop yields based on historical data, weather conditions, and soil health, helping farmers plan and optimize their operations.

Examples:
- **Prospera**: Prospera's AI platform analyzes data from sensors and satellite imagery to predict crop yields and optimize farm management practices.

- **AgriMetis**: AgriMetis uses AI to predict crop yields and recommend optimal planting and harvesting times, improving overall farm productivity.

AI in Entertainment

The entertainment industry leverages AI to create engaging content, enhance user experiences, and personalize recommendations. Here are some key applications of AI in entertainment:

Content Creation

AI assists in creating content such as music, art, and stories, enabling new forms of artistic expression.

Examples:
- **OpenAI's GPT-3**: GPT-3 generates human-like text, enabling applications such as story writing, script generation, and chatbots.

- **AIVA**: AIVA (Artificial Intelligence Virtual Artist) composes music, creating original pieces for various applications, from soundtracks to advertising.

Personalized Recommendations

AI analyzes user preferences to recommend personalized content, keeping users engaged and encouraging them to explore new content.

Examples:
- **Netflix**: Netflix uses AI to recommend movies and TV shows based on users' viewing history and preferences, enhancing user engagement and retention.

- **Spotify**: Spotify's AI-powered recommendation engine suggests songs and playlists based on users' listening habits, helping them discover new music.

Interactive Experiences

AI powers interactive experiences such as virtual reality (VR) and augmented reality (AR), creating immersive and engaging environments.

Examples:
- **Unity**: Unity uses AI to enhance VR and AR experiences, creating realistic and interactive environments for gaming and simulations.

- **Niantic**: Niantic's AI-powered AR platform powers games like Pokémon GO, providing users with interactive and immersive experiences.

Chapter 7: Applications of AI

Introduction

Artificial Intelligence (AI) continues to evolve at a rapid pace, with new applications and innovations emerging regularly. This chapter explores the latest applications of AI, highlighting cutting-edge examples and emerging trends that demonstrate the diverse capabilities of AI technology. From creative endeavors to climate change mitigation, these examples showcase the vast potential of AI in solving complex problems and enhancing various aspects of our lives.

Generative AI in Art and Content Creation

Generative AI refers to AI systems that can create new content, such as images, music, and text. These systems leverage advanced algorithms, such as Generative Adversarial Networks (GANs) and transformer models, to generate content that is often indistinguishable from human-created work.

Examples of Generative AI

- **DALL-E 2 by OpenAI**: DALL-E 2 is a generative AI model that can create realistic images from textual descriptions. For example, given the prompt "a two-story pink house shaped like a shoe," DALL-E 2 can generate a highly detailed and imaginative image that matches the description.

- **ChatGPT by OpenAI**: ChatGPT is a conversational AI model that can generate human-like text based on a given prompt. It is used in various applications, from virtual assistants and customer support to creative writing and educational tools.

- **AIVA (Artificial Intelligence Virtual Artist)**: AIVA is an AI composer that creates original music. It is used in a range of applications, from generating background music for videos and games to composing symphonic pieces for orchestras.

AI in Climate Change Mitigation

AI is playing a crucial role in addressing climate change by optimizing energy use, predicting weather patterns, and modeling the impacts of environmental policies.

Examples of AI in Climate Change

- **Climate Prediction**: AI models, such as those developed by IBM and Microsoft, analyze vast amounts of climate data to predict weather patterns and extreme weather events. These predictions help governments and organizations prepare for and mitigate the impacts of climate change.

- **Energy Optimization**: Companies like Google and Siemens use AI to optimize energy consumption in data centers and smart grids. AI algorithms analyze energy usage patterns and adjust operations to reduce energy consumption and carbon emissions.

- **Environmental Monitoring**: AI-powered drones and satellites monitor environmental conditions, such as deforestation, air quality, and ocean health. Projects like Global Forest Watch use AI to analyze satellite imagery and detect illegal deforestation activities in real time.

AI in Education

AI is transforming education by providing personalized learning experiences, automating administrative tasks, and enhancing student engagement.

Examples of AI in Education

- **Personalized Learning Platforms**: Platforms like Khan Academy and Coursera use AI to tailor educational content to individual students' needs, preferences, and learning styles. This personalized approach helps students achieve better outcomes and stay engaged with their studies.

- **AI Tutors**: AI-powered tutoring systems, such as Carnegie Learning and Squirrel AI, provide personalized assistance and feedback to students. These systems adapt to each student's learning pace and provide targeted support to help them master complex subjects.

- **Administrative Automation**: AI systems, like those developed by AdmitHub and Ivy.ai, automate administrative tasks such as admissions, scheduling, and student support. This reduces the workload for educators and administrative staff, allowing them to focus on teaching and student engagement.

AI in Agriculture

AI is revolutionizing agriculture by improving crop yields, optimizing resource use, and enhancing sustainability.

Examples of AI in Agriculture

- **Precision Agriculture**: AI-powered platforms like Blue River Technology use computer vision and machine learning to monitor crop health, detect weeds, and optimize the application of fertilizers and pesticides. This leads to higher crop yields and reduced environmental impact.

- **Predictive Analytics**: Companies like Climate Corp use AI to analyze historical weather data, soil conditions, and crop performance to predict future yields and recommend optimal planting and harvesting times.

- **Automated Farming Equipment**: AI-driven machinery, such as John Deere's autonomous tractors, perform tasks like planting, harvesting, and soil analysis with high precision. This reduces labor costs and increases efficiency in farming operations.

AI in Healthcare

AI continues to make significant strides in healthcare, improving diagnostics, treatment planning, and patient care.

Examples of AI in Healthcare

- **Early Disease Detection**: AI algorithms developed by companies like PathAI and Zebra Medical Vision analyze medical images to detect diseases such as cancer and heart conditions at early stages. These systems provide accurate and timely diagnoses, improving patient outcomes.

- **Personalized Treatment**: AI platforms like Tempus and IBM Watson for Oncology analyze patient data and medical literature to recommend personalized treatment plans. This approach helps doctors tailor therapies to individual patients, increasing the effectiveness of treatments.

- **Telemedicine**: AI-powered telemedicine platforms, such as Babylon Health and Teladoc, provide virtual consultations and remote patient monitoring. These platforms use AI to analyze patient symptoms and medical history, offering timely medical advice and reducing the need for in-person visits.

AI in Autonomous Vehicles

AI is driving the development of autonomous vehicles, enhancing road safety, and transforming transportation.

Examples of AI in Autonomous Vehicles

- **Self-Driving Cars**: Companies like Tesla and Waymo are at the forefront of developing self-driving cars that use AI to navigate roads, avoid obstacles, and make real-time driving decisions. These vehicles aim to reduce accidents caused by human error and improve overall road safety.

- **Fleet Management**: AI systems like those developed by Nuro and Embark optimize logistics and delivery operations. Autonomous delivery vehicles and trucks use AI to plan efficient routes, reducing fuel consumption and delivery times.

- **Public Transportation**: AI is being used to improve public transportation systems. For example, AI algorithms optimize bus and train schedules based on real-time passenger data, reducing wait times and improving service efficiency.

AI in Finance

AI is transforming the finance industry by enhancing security, improving decision-making, and providing personalized financial services.

Examples of AI in Finance

- **Fraud Detection**: AI systems developed by companies like Darktrace and Palantir analyze transaction data to detect fraudulent activities in real time. These systems use machine learning to identify unusual patterns and prevent financial losses.

- **Robo-Advisors**: AI-powered robo-advisors, such as Betterment and Wealthfront, provide personalized investment advice and portfolio management. These platforms analyze market data and individual risk profiles to recommend optimal investment strategies.

- **Credit Scoring**: AI algorithms developed by companies like ZestFinance and Upstart analyze a wide range of data to assess creditworthiness. This approach enables more accurate credit scoring and expands access to financial services for underserved populations.

AI in Entertainment

AI is enhancing the entertainment industry by creating engaging content, personalizing recommendations, and enabling interactive experiences.

Examples of AI in Entertainment

- **Content Creation**: AI systems like OpenAI's GPT-3 and DeepArt create original content, from written stories and scripts to visual art and music. These systems enable new forms of creative expression and collaboration between humans and machines.

- **Recommendation Engines**: Streaming services like Netflix and Spotify use AI to recommend personalized content based on users' preferences and viewing or listening habits. This keeps users engaged and encourages them to explore new content.

- **Interactive Experiences**: AI powers interactive experiences in virtual reality (VR) and augmented reality (AR). Companies like Unity and Niantic create immersive environments and games that adapt to users' actions, providing dynamic and engaging experiences.

AI in Legal Services

AI is transforming the legal industry by automating routine tasks, enhancing legal research, and improving access to justice.

Examples of AI in Legal Services

- **Document Review**: AI systems like those developed by Relativity and Kira Systems automate the review of legal documents, contracts, and case files. This speeds up the discovery process and reduces the workload for legal professionals.

- **Legal Research**: AI-powered platforms like ROSS Intelligence and Casetext use natural language processing to analyze legal texts and provide relevant case law, statutes, and legal opinions. This helps lawyers find pertinent information quickly and efficiently.

- **Access to Justice**: AI chatbots and virtual assistants, such as DoNotPay and LegalZoom, provide legal advice and assistance to individuals who cannot afford traditional legal services. These tools help users navigate legal processes and access justice more easily.

AI in Human Resources

AI is transforming human resources (HR) by automating recruitment processes, enhancing employee engagement, and improving talent management.

Examples of AI in Human Resources

- **Recruitment and Hiring**: AI-powered platforms like HireVue and Pymetrics analyze candidate data and conduct video interviews to identify the best candidates for job openings. These systems use machine learning to evaluate skills, experience, and cultural fit, streamlining the hiring process.

- **Employee Engagement**: AI-driven tools like Glint and Culture Amp monitor employee sentiment and engagement through surveys and feedback analysis. These insights help HR teams address issues and improve workplace culture.

- **Talent Management**: AI systems like Workday and SAP SuccessFactors use predictive analytics to identify high-potential employees, plan career development paths, and optimize workforce planning. This helps organizations retain top talent and improve overall productivity.

-

Chapter 8: History and Evolution of AI

Introduction

The field of Artificial Intelligence (AI) has a rich history that spans several decades, marked by periods of intense progress and intermittent setbacks. This chapter delves into the history and evolution of AI, tracing its development from early conceptualizations to the advanced technologies of today. By understanding the historical context, we can better appreciate the achievements and challenges that have shaped the AI landscape.

Early Concepts and Foundations

The idea of creating intelligent machines can be traced back to ancient myths and stories. However, the formal foundation of AI as a scientific discipline began in the mid-20th century.

Ancient Myths and Automata

- **Mythological Roots**: Ancient civilizations, including the Greeks and Egyptians, told stories of artificial beings endowed with intelligence or consciousness by master craftsmen and deities.

- **Mechanical Automata**: Throughout history, inventors created mechanical automata that could perform simple tasks, such as the mechanical birds and animals designed by the Greek engineer Hero of Alexandria.

Early 20th Century: Theoretical Foundations

- **Alan Turing and the Turing Machine**: In the 1930s, British mathematician Alan Turing introduced the concept of the Turing Machine, a theoretical model of computation that laid the groundwork for modern computer science and AI.
- **Norbert Wiener and Cybernetics**: In the 1940s, Norbert Wiener developed the field of cybernetics, which explored the principles of feedback and control in machines and living organisms.

The Birth of AI: 1950s and 1960s

The formal inception of AI as a field of study occurred in the 1950s, with several key milestones and pioneering projects.

- **Mechanical Automata**: Throughout history, inventors created mechanical automata that could perform simple tasks, such as the mechanical birds and animals designed by the Greek engineer Hero of Alexandria.

Early 20th Century: Theoretical Foundations

- **Alan Turing and the Turing Machine**: In the 1930s, British mathematician Alan Turing introduced the concept of the Turing Machine, a theoretical model of computation that laid the groundwork for modern computer science and AI.
- **Norbert Wiener and Cybernetics**: In the 1940s, Norbert Wiener developed the field of cybernetics, which explored the principles of feedback and control in machines and living organisms.

The Birth of AI: 1950s and 1960s

The formal inception of AI as a field of study occurred in the 1950s, with several key milestones and pioneering projects.

Dartmouth Conference: 1956

- **The Dartmouth Workshop**: In 1956, John McCarthy, Marvin Minsky, Nathaniel Rochester, and Claude Shannon organized the Dartmouth Conference, which is considered the founding event of AI as a research discipline. The conference aimed to explore the possibility of creating "thinking machines."

- **Coining the Term "Artificial Intelligence"**: John McCarthy is credited with coining the term "artificial intelligence" during the Dartmouth Conference.

Early AI Programs and Milestones

- **Logic Theorist (1955-1956)**: Created by Allen Newell and Herbert A. Simon, the Logic Theorist was one of the first AI programs. It was designed to prove mathematical theorems and is considered the "first artificial intelligence program."

- **General Problem Solver (1957)**: Newell and Simon developed the General Problem Solver (GPS), a program designed to solve a wide range of problems using a heuristic approach.

- **ELIZA (1964-1966)**: Developed by Joseph Weizenbaum, ELIZA was an early natural language processing program that simulated a conversation with a psychotherapist. ELIZA demonstrated the potential of AI in human-computer interaction.

The Rise and Fall of AI: 1970s and 1980s

The 1970s and 1980s saw both significant advancements and notable challenges in the field of AI.

Early Enthusiasm and Research

- **Expert Systems**: The development of expert systems, such as DENDRAL (for chemical analysis) and MYCIN (for medical diagnosis), marked a significant advancement in AI. These systems used rule-based approaches to solve complex problems in specific domains.

- **Prolog and Lisp**: The programming languages Prolog and Lisp became popular for AI research due to their suitability for symbolic reasoning and problem-solving.

The First AI Winter

- **Overpromising and Underperformance**: Despite early successes, many AI projects failed to deliver on their ambitious promises. This led to growing skepticism and reduced funding for AI research.

- **The Lighthill Report (1973)**: The Lighthill Report, commissioned by the British government, criticized the progress and feasibility of AI research, leading to a decline in funding and interest. This period of reduced AI activity is known as the "AI Winter."

The Resurgence of AI: 1990s and 2000s

AI experienced a resurgence in the 1990s and 2000s, driven by advancements in machine learning, increased computational power, and the availability of large datasets.

Breakthroughs and Innovations
- **Deep Blue (1997)**: IBM's Deep Blue made history by defeating world chess champion Garry Kasparov in a six-game match. This milestone demonstrated the potential of AI in strategic game playing.

- **Support Vector Machines (SVMs)**: The development of SVMs and other advanced machine learning algorithms improved the accuracy and performance of AI systems in various tasks, including image recognition and natural language processing.

The Rise of Big Data and Machine Learning

- **Internet and Data Explosion**: The proliferation of the internet and digital technologies generated vast amounts of data, providing the fuel needed for training machine learning models.

- **Algorithmic Advancements**: Researchers developed new algorithms, such as decision trees, ensemble methods, and neural networks, that could handle large datasets and complex patterns.

The Deep Learning Revolution: 2010s

The 2010s witnessed a revolution in AI driven by deep learning, a subset of machine learning that uses neural networks with many layers to model complex patterns in data.

Key Developments and Achievements

- **ImageNet and AlexNet (2012)**: The ImageNet competition, which involved classifying millions of images into thousands of categories, spurred advancements in deep learning. AlexNet, a deep convolutional neural network, achieved a breakthrough performance in the competition, demonstrating the power of deep learning.

- **AlphaGo (2016)**: DeepMind's AlphaGo made headlines by defeating world champion Go player Lee Sedol. Go is a complex board game with a vast number of possible moves, and AlphaGo's success showcased the capabilities of deep reinforcement learning.

Expansion of AI Applications

- **Natural Language Processing**: The development of transformer models, such as BERT (Bidirectional Encoder Representations from Transformers) and GPT (Generative Pre-trained Transformer), revolutionized natural language processing, enabling more accurate language understanding and generation.

- **Autonomous Systems**: Advances in computer vision, robotics, and machine learning enabled the development of autonomous systems, such as self-driving cars and drones.

The Present and Future of AI

AI continues to evolve rapidly, with ongoing research and development pushing the boundaries of what is possible.

Current Trends and Innovations

- **AI in Healthcare**: AI is being used to develop new diagnostic tools, personalized treatments, and predictive analytics for disease prevention and management.

- **Generative AI**: Generative models, such as GANs and VAEs, are being used to create realistic images, music, and text, opening up new possibilities in creative industries.

- **Ethical AI**: Researchers and organizations are increasingly focused on ensuring the ethical use of AI, addressing issues such as bias, transparency, and accountability.

Future Directions and Challenges

- **Artificial General Intelligence (AGI)**: While current AI systems excel in specific tasks, achieving AGI—machines with human-like cognitive abilities—remains a long-term goal and significant challenge.

- **AI Governance and Regulation**: As AI becomes more integrated into society, there is a growing need for robust governance frameworks and regulations to ensure its safe and ethical use.

- **Human-AI Collaboration**: The future of AI will likely involve greater collaboration between humans and machines, enhancing human capabilities and creating new opportunities for innovation.

The history and evolution of AI is a testament to the enduring quest for intelligent machines and the remarkable progress that has been made over the decades. From early theoretical foundations to the deep learning revolution, AI has come a long way, transforming various aspects of our lives and industries. As we look to the future, continued research, innovation, and ethical considerations will be essential to harness the full potential of AI and ensure its benefits are shared broadly across society.

Chapter 9: Ethical Use of AI

Introduction

As AI technology becomes increasingly integrated into various aspects of our lives, it is crucial to consider the ethical implications and responsibilities associated with its development and deployment. This chapter examines the principles and practices that guide the ethical use of AI, addressing issues such as bias, transparency, accountability, and the broader societal impact of AI systems.

Principles of Ethical AI

Several core principles underpin the ethical use of AI, providing a framework for responsible development and deployment.

Fairness and Non-Discrimination

- **Addressing Bias**: AI systems must be designed and trained to minimize bias and ensure fair treatment for all individuals. This involves using diverse and representative datasets, as well as implementing techniques to detect and mitigate bias in AI models.

- **Inclusive Design**: AI should be developed with consideration for diverse user groups, ensuring that the technology is accessible and beneficial to everyone, regardless of their background or characteristics.

Transparency and Explainability

- **Transparent Processes**: AI development and deployment processes should be transparent, providing clear information about how AI systems are designed, trained, and used. This includes documentation of data sources, algorithms,and decision-making processes.

- **Explainable AI**: AI systems should be designed to provide explanations for their decisions and actions. Explainable AI helps build trust and allows users to understand and challenge the outcomes produced by AI systems, ensuring accountability.

Accountability and Responsibility

- Clear Accountability: Developers, organizations, and users must have clear accountability for the outcomes produced by AI systems. This includes assigning responsibility for the design, deployment, and maintenance of AI systems, as well as establishing mechanisms for addressing grievances and disputes.

- **Ethical Oversight**: Organizations should implement ethical oversight structures, such as ethics boards or review committees, to oversee AI projects and ensure they align with ethical principles and societal values.

Privacy and Security

- **Data Privacy**: AI systems should respect individuals' privacy rights by implementing robust data protection measures. This includes obtaining informed consent for data collection and ensuring that personal data is stored and processed securely.

- **Security Measures**: AI systems must be designed with strong security measures to protect against unauthorized access, data breaches, and malicious attacks. Ensuring the integrity and confidentiality of data is critical for maintaining trust in AI technologies.

Societal and Environmental Impact

- **Social Good**: AI should be developed and deployed with consideration for its broader societal impact, prioritizing applications that promote social good and address pressing global challenges.

- **Sustainability**: The environmental impact of AI technologies, including their energy consumption and carbon footprint, should be minimized through sustainable practices and the development of energy-efficient algorithms and hardware.

Addressing Bias and Fairness

Bias in AI systems can lead to unfair and discriminatory outcomes, exacerbating existing inequalities. Addressing bias is a critical aspect of ethical AI development.

Sources of Bias

- **Data Bias**: Bias can be introduced through the data used to train AI models. If the training data is not representative of the diverse populations the AI system will serve, the resulting model may produce biased outcomes.

- **Algorithmic Bias**: Bias can also arise from the design of the algorithms themselves. Certain algorithmic choices or assumptions may inadvertently favor one group over another.

- **Human Bias**: Bias in AI systems can reflect the biases of the humans involved in their development, including data collectors, annotators, and developers.

Mitigating Bias

- **Diverse and Representative Data**: Ensuring that training data is diverse and representative of the populations the AI system will serve is crucial for minimizing bias. This includes collecting data from various sources and demographic groups.

- **Bias Detection and Mitigation**: Implementing techniques to detect and mitigate bias in AI models is essential. This may involve using fairness metrics, bias mitigation algorithms, and regular audits to identify and address bias.

- **Human-in-the-Loop**: Incorporating human judgment in the AI decision-making process can help identify and correct biased outcomes. Human oversight ensures that AI systems are held to ethical standards and can intervene when biases are detected.

Ensuring Transparency and Explainability

Transparency and explainability are key principles for building trust in AI systems and ensuring they operate ethically.

Techniques for Explainable AI

- **Interpretable Models**: Using interpretable models, such as decision trees and linear regression, can enhance explainability by providing clear and understandable decision-making processes.

- **Post-Hoc Explanations**: For complex models, such as deep neural networks, post-hoc explanation techniques, such as LIME (Local Interpretable Model-Agnostic Explanations) and SHAP (SHapley Additive exPlanations), can provide insights into how the model arrived at its decisions.

- **Visualization Tools**: Visualization tools, such as feature importance plots and decision maps, can help users understand the factors influencing AI decisions and identify potential biases or errors.

Benefits of Explainable AI

- **Building Trust**: Explainable AI helps build trust by providing users with clear and understandable explanations for AI decisions, fostering confidence in the technology.

- **Improving Accountability**: Providing explanations for AI decisions enhances accountability by allowing users to understand and challenge the outcomes, ensuring that AI systems are held to ethical standards.

- **Facilitating Regulation**: Explainable AI supports regulatory compliance by providing transparency and traceability in AI decision-making processes, helping organizations meet legal and ethical requirements.

Promoting Accountability and Responsibility

Ensuring accountability and responsibility in AI development and deployment is critical for ethical AI practices.

Mechanisms for Accountability

- **Ethical Guidelines and Standards**: Developing and adhering to ethical guidelines and industry standards for AI development helps ensure that AI systems are designed and deployed responsibly.

- **Ethics Boards and Committees**: Establishing ethics boards or review committees within organizations provides oversight for AI projects, ensuring they align with ethical principles and societal values.

- **Regulatory Frameworks**: Governments and regulatory bodies should establish frameworks for AI governance, providing clear guidelines and regulations to ensure responsible AI development and deployment.

Case Studies in Accountability

- **IBM's AI Ethics Board**: IBM has established an AI Ethics Board to oversee its AI initiatives, ensuring they align with ethical principles and address societal concerns. The board reviews AI projects and provides guidance on ethical issues.

- **Google's AI Principles**: Google has developed a set of AI principles that guide its AI development, emphasizing fairness, transparency, privacy, and accountability. The principles serve as a framework for responsible AI practices within the company.

Protecting Privacy and Security

Privacy and security are fundamental considerations for ethical AI, ensuring that individuals' rights are respected and data is protected.

Privacy Protection Measures

- **Data Anonymization**: Anonymizing personal data helps protect individuals' privacy by removing identifying information, making it difficult to trace data back to specific individuals.

- **Informed Consent**: Obtaining informed consent from individuals for data collection and processing ensures that they are aware of and agree to how their data will be used.

- **Data Minimization**: Collecting only the data necessary for a specific purpose reduces the risk of privacy breaches and limits the amount of sensitive information stored and processed.

Security Measures

- **Encryption**: Encrypting data during storage and transmission protects it from unauthorized access and breaches, ensuring the confidentiality and integrity of sensitive information.

- **Access Controls**: Implementing robust access controls restricts access to sensitive data and AI systems to authorized personnel only, reducing the risk of unauthorized use or tampering.

- **Regular Audits**: Conducting regular security audits and assessments helps identify vulnerabilities and ensures that AI systems and data are protected against emerging threats.

Assessing Societal and Environmental Impact

AI has the potential to significantly impact society and the environment, and it is essential to consider these impacts when developing and deploying AI systems.

Societal Impact

- **Economic Displacement**: AI can automate jobs, leading to potential economic displacement and unemployment. Addressing this impact requires investing in education and retraining programs to help workers transition to new roles.

- **Digital Divide**: Ensuring equitable access to AI technology is critical for preventing a digital divide, where certain groups may be left behind due to lack of access or resources.

- **Social Equity**: AI should be developed and deployed in ways that promote social equity, addressing disparities and ensuring that the benefits of AI are shared broadly across society.

Environmental Impact

- **Energy Consumption**: AI systems, particularly those involving deep learning and large-scale computations, can consume significant amounts of energy. Developing energy-efficient algorithms and hardware can help mitigate this impact.

- **Sustainable Practices**: Incorporating sustainable practices in AI development, such as using renewable energy sources and optimizing resource use, helps reduce the environmental footprint of AI technologies.

The ethical use of AI is essential for ensuring that AI technologies are developed and deployed responsibly, with consideration for fairness, transparency, accountability, privacy, security, and societal impact. By adhering to ethical principles and implementing best practices, we can harness the benefits of AI while minimizing potential harms and ensuring that AI serves the greater good.

Chapter 10: The Future of AI: What to Expect in the Next 5 Years

Introduction

Artificial Intelligence (AI) is poised to continue its rapid evolution, with significant advancements and innovations expected in the coming years. This chapter explores the future of AI, highlighting key trends, emerging technologies, and potential developments that will shape the AI landscape over the next five years. From advancements in machine learning to new applications and ethical considerations, we will examine what to expect as AI continues to transform various aspects of our lives.

Advancements in Machine Learning and Deep Learning

Machine learning and deep learning are at the forefront of AI research, driving many of the recent breakthroughs. In the next five years, we can expect several advancements in these areas.

Improved Algorithms and Models

- **Efficiency and Scalability**: Researchers will continue to develop more efficient and scalable algorithms that can handle larger datasets and more complex tasks. This includes advancements in neural network architectures, optimization techniques, and training methods.

- **Transfer Learning**: Transfer learning, where models pre-trained on large datasets are fine-tuned for specific tasks, will become more prevalent. This approach reduces the need for vast amounts of labeled data and accelerates the development of AI applications.

- **Few-Shot and Zero-Shot Learning**: Techniques that enable models to learn from a few examples (few-shot learning) or without any examples (zero-shot learning) will improve, making AI more adaptable and capable of handling a wider range of tasks.

Integration of AI and Edge Computing

- **Edge AI**: The integration of AI with edge computing will become more widespread, enabling AI applications to run directly on devices such as smartphones, IoT devices, and autonomous systems. Edge AI reduces latency, enhances privacy, and lowers the dependency on cloud infrastructure.

- **Federated Learning**: Federated learning, which allows AI models to be trained across multiple decentralized devices without sharing raw data, will see increased adoption. This approach improves privacy and data security while enabling collaborative model training.

Emerging Applications and Innovations

The next five years will witness the emergence of new AI applications and innovations across various industries, enhancing efficiency, solving complex problems, and creating new opportunities.

AI in Healthcare

- **Advanced Diagnostics**: AI-powered diagnostic tools will become more sophisticated, capable of analyzing diverse data sources, including genetic information, medical images, and electronic health records, to provide accurate and early diagnoses.

- **Precision Medicine**: AI will play a crucial role in the development of precision medicine, tailoring treatments to individual patients based on their unique genetic makeup and health profiles.

- **Telehealth and Remote Monitoring**: The integration of AI in telehealth platforms will enhance remote patient monitoring, enabling continuous health assessments and timely interventions.

AI in Transportation

- **Autonomous Vehicles**: The development and deployment of autonomous vehicles will accelerate, with significant advancements in safety, navigation, and decision-making capabilities. This will include not only self-driving cars but also autonomous trucks, drones, and delivery robots.

- **Smart Traffic Management**: AI-powered traffic management systems will optimize traffic flow, reduce congestion, and improve public transportation efficiency through real-time data analysis and predictive modeling.

- **Hyperloop and High-Speed Rail**: AI will be instrumental in the development and operation of next-generation transportation systems, such as Hyperloop and high-speed rail, enhancing safety and efficiency.

AI in Finance

- **Predictive Analytics**: Financial institutions will increasingly use AI for predictive analytics, helping them forecast market trends, assess risks, and make informed investment decisions.

- **Automated Trading**: AI-driven trading algorithms will become more sophisticated, capable of executing trades with higher precision and speed, while managing risks more effectively.

- **Customer Service**: AI-powered chatbots and virtual assistants will enhance customer service in the financial sector, providing personalized advice and support.

AI in Retail

- **Personalized Shopping**: AI will further personalize the shopping experience by analyzing customer preferences and behaviors to recommend products and services tailored to individual needs.

- **Supply Chain Optimization**: AI will optimize supply chain operations, improving demand forecasting, inventory management, and logistics to reduce costs and enhance efficiency.

- **Augmented Reality (AR) Shopping**: The integration of AI and AR will create immersive shopping experiences, allowing customers to visualize products in real-time before making a purchase.

Ethical Considerations and AI Governance

As AI continues to evolve, ethical considerations and robust governance frameworks will become increasingly important to ensure responsible development and deployment.

AI Ethics and Fairness

- **Bias Mitigation**: Continued efforts will be made to detect and mitigate biases in AI systems, ensuring fairness and equity in AI applications.

- **Transparency and Explainability**: Enhancing transparency and explainability in AI decision-making processes will be a priority, helping build trust and accountability.

- **Inclusive Design**: AI development will focus on inclusive design principles, ensuring that AI technologies are accessible and beneficial to diverse populations.

AI Regulation and Policy

- **Global Standards**: International collaboration will be essential in developing global standards and regulations for AI, ensuring consistency and addressing cross-border challenges.

- **AI Auditing and Compliance**: Regulatory frameworks will include requirements for AI auditing and compliance, ensuring that AI systems adhere to ethical guidelines and legal standards.

- **Public Engagement**: Engaging the public in discussions about AI ethics and governance will be crucial for building societal trust and ensuring that AI development aligns with public values and expectations.

Future Directions in AI Research

AI research will continue to explore new frontiers, pushing the boundaries of what is possible and addressing some of the most challenging problems in the field.

Artificial General Intelligence (AGI)

- **Cognitive Architectures**: Researchers will explore advanced cognitive architectures and models inspired by human cognition, aiming to develop AGI systems capable of generalizing knowledge across diverse tasks.

- **Learning Paradigms**: New learning paradigms, such as lifelong learning and meta-learning, will be investigated to enable AI systems to continuously learn and adapt over time.

- **Ethical AGI**: Ensuring that AGI systems are developed with robust ethical frameworks will be a critical area of research, addressing potential risks and societal impacts.

Human-AI Collaboration

- **Augmented Intelligence**: AI systems will be designed to augment human intelligence, enhancing decision-making, creativity, and problem-solving capabilities through collaborative interactions.

- **Human-Centered AI**: Research will focus on developing AI technologies that prioritize human values, needs, and well-being, ensuring that AI complements and supports human activities.

- **Intuitive Interfaces**: Advances in natural language processing, computer vision, and haptic feedback will create more intuitive and seamless interfaces for human-AI interaction.

The future of AI promises exciting advancements and innovations that will transform various aspects of our lives. From healthcare and transportation to finance and retail, AI will continue to enhance efficiency, solve complex problems, and create new opportunities. However, the ethical and responsible development of AI will be paramount to ensuring that these technologies benefit society as a whole. By addressing ethical considerations, establishing robust governance frameworks, and fostering human-AI collaboration, we can harness the full potential of AI and shape a future where AI technologies contribute to the greater good.

Chapter 11: AI Facts and Figures

Introduction

Artificial Intelligence (AI) is a rapidly evolving field with significant implications for various industries and aspects of daily life. This chapter presents a collection of interesting facts and figures about AI, offering insights into its current state, growth trends, and impact across different sectors. These statistics highlight the transformative potential of AI and underscore the importance of continued research, development, and ethical considerations.

Global AI Market and Investment

Market Growth

- **Global Market Size**: The global AI market is projected to grow from USD 93.5 billion in 2021 to USD 997.77 billion by 2028, at a compound annual growth rate (CAGR) of 40.2% during the forecast period.

-

- **Regional Leaders**: North America currently leads the AI market, followed by Europe and Asia-Pacific. The Asia-Pacific region is expected to experience the highest growth rate due to increasing AI adoption in countries like China, Japan, and India.

Investment Trends

- **Venture Capital Funding**: In 2020, AI startups received approximately USD 73.4 billion in venture capital funding, reflecting strong investor interest in AI technology and innovation.

- **Corporate Investments**: Major technology companies, including Google, Microsoft, Amazon, and IBM, are making significant investments in AI research and development, driving advancements and commercialization of AI applications.

AI Adoption Across Industries

Healthcare

- **Market Size**: The AI in healthcare market is expected to reach USD 45.2 billion by 2026, growing at a CAGR of 44.9% from 2021.

- **AI Applications**: Key applications of AI in healthcare include medical imaging, diagnostics, personalized medicine, drug discovery, and remote patient monitoring.

Finance

- **Cost Savings**: AI is projected to save the banking industry USD 447 billion by 2023, through efficiencies in fraud detection, risk management, customer service, and trading.

- **Adoption Rate**: Approximately 77% of financial institutions are expected to adopt AI solutions by 2023, driven by the need for improved decision-making and operational efficiency.

Retail

- **Revenue Impact**: AI is expected to increase retail revenue by USD 290 billion by 2025, through personalized recommendations, inventory management, and customer service enhancements.

- **AI Integration**: About 45% of retailers are using AI to enhance customer experiences and streamline operations, with significant growth anticipated in the coming years.

Transportation

- **Autonomous Vehicles**: The autonomous vehicle market is projected to reach USD 556.67 billion by 2026, growing at a CAGR of 39.47% from 2021.

- **AI Applications**: AI is used in self-driving cars, fleet management, traffic optimization, and predictive maintenance, improving safety and efficiency in transportation.

AI Research and Development

Academic Research

- **Publications**: The number of AI-related research publications has increased significantly, with over 1.2 million AI research papers published between 2015 and 2020.

- **Top Institutions**: Leading academic institutions in AI research include Stanford University, Massachusetts Institute of Technology (MIT), Carnegie Mellon University, and the University of California, Berkeley.

AI Patents

- **Patent Filings**: The number of AI-related patent filings has surged, with over 340,000 AI patents filed globally between 2010 and 2020.

- **Top Filers**: Companies like IBM, Microsoft, Google, and Samsung are among the top filers of AI patents, reflecting their commitment to innovation and technology leadership.

AI Workforce and Skills

Job Market

- **Job Growth**: The demand for AI professionals is growing rapidly, with AI-related job postings increasing by 119% between 2018 and 2020.

- **Top Roles**: In-demand AI roles include machine learning engineers, data scientists, AI researchers, and AI ethics specialists.

Skills and Education

- **Skill Demand**: Key skills required for AI roles include proficiency in programming languages (such as Python and R), knowledge of machine learning frameworks (such as TensorFlow and PyTorch), and expertise in data analysis and statistical modeling.

- **Educational Programs**: Universities and online learning platforms are increasingly offering specialized AI courses and degree programs to meet the growing demand for AI expertise. Notable programs include Stanford University's AI specialization, MIT's Professional Certificate in Machine Learning and Artificial Intelligence, and Coursera's AI for Everyone course by Andrew Ng.

- **Regulatory Frameworks**: Countries around the world are working on regulatory frameworks to govern the use of AI. The European Union's proposed AI Act aims to create a harmonized legal framework for AI, addressing issues such as transparency, accountability, and safety.

AI in Everyday Life

Consumer Electronics

- **Smart Assistants**: AI-powered smart assistants like Amazon's Alexa, Apple's Siri, and Google Assistant are becoming increasingly integrated into everyday life, helping users with tasks such as setting reminders, controlling smart home devices, and answering queries.

- **Wearable Technology**: AI is embedded in wearable devices, such as smartwatches and fitness trackers, to monitor health metrics, provide personalized fitness recommendations, and detect anomalies.

Social Media

- **Content Recommendation**: Social media platforms like Facebook, Instagram, and TikTok use AI algorithms to recommend content, personalize user feeds, and enhance user engagement.

- **Content Moderation**: AI is used for content moderation, detecting and removing inappropriate or harmful content to ensure a safer online environment.

Home Automation

- **Smart Home Devices**: AI-powered smart home devices, such as thermostats, security cameras, and lighting systems, provide enhanced convenience, energy efficiency, and security for homeowners.

- **Voice Control**: AI-enabled voice control systems allow users to interact with their smart home devices through natural language commands, making home automation more accessible and user-friendly.

Interesting AI Milestones

Historical Achievements

- **Deep Blue Defeats Kasparov (1997)**: IBM's Deep Blue became the first computer to defeat a reigning world chess champion, Garry Kasparov, in a six-game match.

- **AlphaGo Defeats Lee Sedol (2016)**: DeepMind's AlphaGo defeated world champion Go player Lee Sedol in a historic match, demonstrating the potential of deep reinforcement learning.

Recent Breakthroughs

- **GPT-3 (2020)**: OpenAI's GPT-3, a state-of-the-art language model, demonstrated remarkable capabilities in natural language understanding and generation, setting new benchmarks in AI research.

- **AlphaFold (2020)**: DeepMind's AlphaFold made a significant breakthrough in protein folding, accurately predicting protein structures and advancing our understanding of biological processes.

Future Prospects and Predictions

AI and the Workforce

- **Job Transformation**: While AI is expected to automate certain tasks, it will also create new job opportunities and transform existing roles. The focus will shift towards tasks that require human creativity, problem-solving, and emotional intelligence.

- **Reskilling and Upskilling**: As AI technology advances, there will be a growing need for reskilling and upskilling programs to help workers adapt to new job requirements and leverage AI tools effectively.

AI and Society

- **Healthcare Revolution**: AI will continue to revolutionize healthcare, enabling early disease detection, personalized treatments, and improved patient outcomes.

- **Sustainable Development**: AI will play a crucial role in addressing global challenges such as climate change, food security, and sustainable development, providing innovative solutions to complex problems.

Technological Advancements

- **Quantum Computing and AI**: The convergence of quantum computing and AI holds the potential to solve computationally intensive problems that are currently beyond the reach of classical computers.

- **Human-AI Collaboration**: The future will see increased collaboration between humans and AI systems, enhancing human capabilities and enabling new forms of creative and intellectual exploration.

Artificial Intelligence is a rapidly evolving field with profound implications for various industries and aspects of daily life. The facts and figures presented in this chapter highlight the significant impact of AI on the global economy, workforce, and society. As AI continues to advance, it is essential to address ethical considerations, ensure responsible development, and harness the technology's potential to create a better future for all.

By understanding the current state of AI, its historical milestones, and future prospects, we can appreciate the transformative power of AI and its role in shaping the world of tomorrow. Through continued research, innovation, and ethical considerations, we can harness the full potential of AI to drive positive change and improve quality of life.